ʀᴏᴍ BARTER ᴛᴏ GOLD

THE STORY OF MONEY

by SOLVEIG PAULSON RUSSELL

illustrated by CARY

 Rand McNally & Company

Chicago   New York   San Francisco

To
David Hansen
and
Ray Gardner

TIME OF NO MONEY

Long long ago, when men lived in caves, there was no money. There was no place to buy anything, because there was no need to buy anything. And so there was no need for money.

In those days, each family found its own food. A man killed wild animals with a stone hammer or some other crude weapon.

Then he dragged the animals to his cave and skinned them. He and his family ate the meat and used the skin for clothing.

Food and clothing, and a cave to live in were all they needed.

As time went on, men began to use their minds more. They learned to make better tools from stones and wood and bone. Some men were better at making tools than others. The men who made the best tools found that they could trade their tools to other men who could not make tools well. They traded tools for meat or other food. They traded for things they wanted and things they needed.

This meant that families no longer had to do everything for themselves. They could do the kind of work they liked best or did especially well and they could trade with others to get different things.

Trading one kind of thing for another is called barter. Even today we barter. We often see advertisements in newspapers from someone who wishes to trade something he has for something he wants. Some time you must have traded something you had for something someone else had. Then you were bartering.

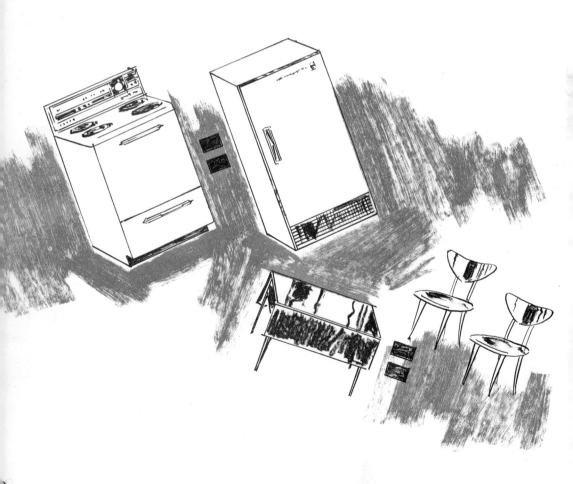

9

Bartering continued for thousands of years after the first cave men began to trade. It continued even after men learned to build houses, and tame animals, and raise crops. It continued even after people began to live together in villages and towns.

As more people made more things, it became harder for them to trade. First a man had to find someone who wanted what he had to trade. If he found someone, that man had to have something the first man wanted in return. A basket maker would have to find people who wanted baskets, and they had to have something to trade that the basket maker needed.

THE FIRST KINDS OF MONEY

At last people decided that it would be easier if they had something that could be exchanged for many things. They wanted something they could use as we use money, though they didn't know the word "money" then.

Anything can be used in this way as long as the people who do the trading agree to the exchange, and as long as it's something that isn't too easy to get. Cattle, salt, furs, rubber, beads, shells, cloth, tea, fish-hooks, and tobacco are just a few of the things that have been

used for money in different parts of the world.

Many years ago anyone who had a great number of cattle was rich. People needed cattle for milk and meat; also their hides could be used for leather.

In those days not only cows and oxen, but sheep and pigs as well were called cattle.

If a man wanted something expensive, like a suit of armor, he would pay for it by driving a herd of cattle to the man who made the armor. Or if a boy needed a new pair of shoes he would have to lead a lamb or sheep to the shoemaker. That kind of money would be quite unhandy for us.

Even in those days, cattle didn't

work out very well, because cattle had
to be fed and cared for. Also there was
a difference in cattle. Some would be fat
and sleek. Some would be thin and old.

When boats were invented, people
began to trade with other countries.
They found that cattle did not make
good money for journeys over water. It
was not easy to move cattle long
distances. Something was needed that
could be moved easily. So grain and
salt were often used. Grain was useful.
It could be divided into small amounts.
It could be carried about, stored, and
saved, and people wanted it.

Salt was also useful. It, too, could be carried and divided easily. It was important to men, as it still is, and in those days it was not easy to get. Salt had to be dried out from sea water or dug from salt mines. Even today salt is used as money by some tribes of Africa.

People have always liked to decorate themselves with things they think are beautiful. Bracelets and necklaces made of shells are good decorations. Shells made good money as well as good decorations because they did not spoil, they were easy to carry, and people wanted them.

Cowrie shells were used in lands around the Indian Ocean, but in America the Indians used clam shells and other shells found here. Our eastern Indians called their shell money "wampum."

Wampum was strung on strings or sewed on clothing. Belts were made of it.

The Indians of the Northwest made polished stone beads that they used for money. Whale teeth, tiger teeth, and claws of animals, as well as unusual and beautiful feathers have been used for money and decorations.

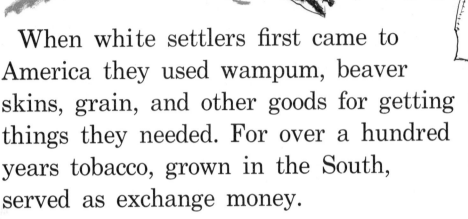

When white settlers first came to America they used wampum, beaver skins, grain, and other goods for getting things they needed. For over a hundred years tobacco, grown in the South, served as exchange money.

METAL BECOMES MONEY

After using cattle, grain, salt, shells, and other things for a long, long time, men finally began to use metal for money. Copper, lead, gold, silver, and tin had been known since the days of early history. Bracelets, necklaces, anklets, and earrings were made of metal. Tools, weapons, and pots were made of metal, too, and these were traded in payment for other goods.

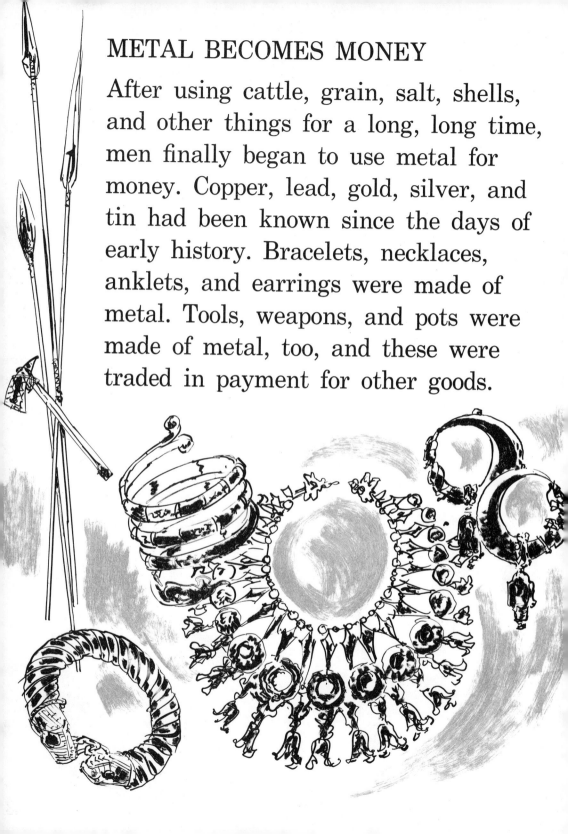

In Greece, at one time, copper pots
were used as money. Everyone wanted a
copper pot instead of one made from
clay. In a famous poem, the *Iliad,*
written about that time, we are told
that a three-legged pot was the first
prize for wrestlers.

Different forms of metal were used by various people in the early days of metal money. The Greeks made their pieces of metal into thin rods. These rods were called "oboli." Several could be held in the hand at one time.

Romans made a rod of copper about a foot long. Egyptians made rods and

rings of heavy metal. Some people used lumps of metal for money.

Lumps, rings, bars, and rods of metal were used for hundreds of years. But they weren't entirely satisfactory, either.

THE FIRST COINS

Some of the rods and rings were very heavy, too heavy to carry around. They had to be weighed to tell how much each was worth because they were not all alike. Sometimes people who were not honest mixed cheaper metal with gold or silver and then said their money was made of solid gold or solid silver.

So at last, thousands of years ago, coins came into use.

At first these coins were just rounded lumps of a mixture of gold and silver. These metals were used because they had more value and were easier to shape than other metals. Also they were pretty and shiny. They were stamped with a mark which told their weight and purity.

The early coins were made by merchants or traders who sometimes were not honest, so the marks could not always be depended upon.

As time passed, the heads of countries took over the coining of money, just as our government does now. The coins were all the same size and weight. This meant they did not have to be weighed each time they were spent.

At first these coins were stamped with simple designs such as forms of fish, cows, and cups. The smooth round piece of metal was placed between two dies, or designs carved in metal molds, and then the top die was struck with a heavy hammer. This made the marks on the dies appear on the coin. Later coins were often stamped with fancy designs.

Four hundred and fifty years before Christ, the Greeks became experts at making coins. They made some of the most beautiful ones ever seen. Their dies had carefully carved heads of gods, goddesses, and Greek images upon them. The Greeks spread the use of coins to many places.

After the Greeks, the Romans made many coins. One of their silver coins, made about 269 years before Christ, was called the "denarius." The Romans stamped these coins with many different kinds of pictures, and they used them for hundreds of years. Some of these coins can be seen in museums. They tell us a lot about the tools and fashions and important events in the lives of the Romans of those days.

The Romans did not have much gold or silver in their own country. In order to spread these metals around their great empire they began to use less and less gold and silver for their coins. They mixed these precious metals with metals of little value. This made the Roman coins worth less; it took more of them to buy things. Prices went up. Trade began to fall off. Greedy people hoarded the gold. For this, and other reasons, Rome became a weaker nation and, finally, about four hundred and fifty years after Christ, tribes of savages overran this once powerful country.

Because the savage tribes took over Europe, the next seven or eight hundred years are recorded in history as the Dark Ages. There was a great deal of poverty and fighting. Learning and art were almost forgotten. Coins were of little value and very few of them were made.

When these hard years ended, money again became important. Trade was carried on and people began to be free to live happier lives. Countries again took up the making of coins, and coin making has continued to our day.

MONEY IN COLONIAL AMERICA

As we mentioned before, the white people who first settled in our country bartered goods. The few coins they brought with them from other lands were soon sent back on ships to buy things they needed.

In exchange for furs, tobacco, flour, and other goods sold to Spanish traders, the colonists were paid partly in Spanish money. The colonists sometimes cut these coins into eight pieces that they called "bits." That is how they got the silver "pieces-of-eight" we read about in pirate stories. The bits were used for change and even today we hear quarters spoken of as "two bits."

Although some coins from other countries found their way to Colonial America, there were not enough of them. So animal skins and land products were used for money just as they had been in times long past.

England refused to let the colonists make their own coins. But in 1652 the people of Massachusetts made coins, anyway, from the silver of Spanish dollars and any other silver that could be found. These coins were stamped with the words "New England" and the picture of a tree. They were the first coins made in America. These coins, too, soon left the country to pay for goods brought from Europe.

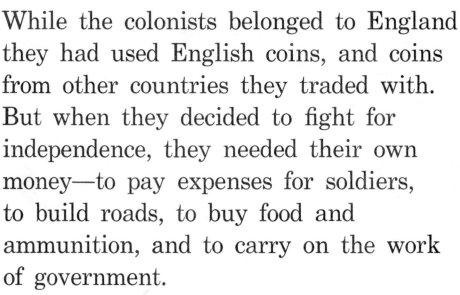

While the colonists belonged to England they had used English coins, and coins from other countries they traded with. But when they decided to fight for independence, they needed their own money—to pay expenses for soldiers, to build roads, to buy food and ammunition, and to carry on the work of government.

The Continental Congress made it lawful for the colonies to issue paper money. These paper bills were just promises to pay. But there was no gold or silver to pay with, so soon the paper money wasn't worth much. By the end of the Revolutionary War it was worth less than two cents for every dollar.

After the war, our new government set up a good money system as soon as possible.

HOW OUR COINS ARE MADE

It took a number of years to do this.
In 1792 our first mint was established.
A mint is a place where coins are made.
The first coins were half dimes, called
dismes, made in 1792 or 1793. These
were followed by one-cent and half-cent
coins.

Ever since then we have been making coins, though they have, of course, changed in design through the years.

All of our coins, dollars, half-dollars, quarters, dimes, nickels, and pennies are made by our government in mints. The United States has had mints in several cities but now there is only one, in Philadelphia.

All coins begin as chunks of metal. Nickel, copper, zinc, tin, and silver are used by our government to make our coins. Two or three of these metals are weighed and put together to make a mixture, or alloy, of metals for coins. Pure silver is too soft for coins. With copper added to it the alloy becomes hard and tough enough to wear well. For all our silver coins we use one part of copper to nine parts of silver.

After the metals are weighed they are heated in great furnaces. The hot gas furnaces melt the metal alloy until it is a boiling liquid.

Then the liquid is poured into molds.
When the alloy is cool it comes from
the molds in the form of bars of metal.

The bars from the molds are then
rolled into thin strips by great machine
rollers.

After they are smoothed out to the right thickness, the strips are cut into rounds by cutters much as cookies are cut from cooky dough. These rounds are called planchets. Many can be punched out or cut at one time by the cutting machine.

The planchets are heated, cleaned, and polished. Then they go through a milling machine that raises a little edge on each one. This edge helps to keep them from wearing out too quickly.

From the milling machine, the planchets go to the coining presses, where each one is stamped on both sides with a design. The designs are pressed into the metal by dies, with a pressure of 100 tons to the square inch.

After being weighed, the new coins are counted by a counting machine and put into bags.

Each year great numbers of coins
are made. And each year many worn-out
coins are returned to the mints to be
melted and made into new coins.

USE AND PROTECTION OF MONEY

Money never rests long in one place. It is always being spent and respent.

Even when you put your money into a savings account in the bank, the bank uses your money in its business. Putting money into a savings account makes you a depositor. The bank adds more money to your money, or pays you interest, as payment for the use of the money. When the bank spends your money, you can be sure you will get back as much as you put in, plus interest, when you need it. The government has made laws to protect depositors that all banks must follow.

The money people have on hand moves quickly from one person to another.

Money is important only for what it can buy, but *what* you buy with it is also important.

Our government used to make gold coins. But now all of our gold is kept in vaults, usually in the form of large bars, about the size of bricks. This is because people used to save gold as they do jewelry, and our government wants money to be used.

The vaults are strong, half-buried buildings with very thick walls, burglar alarms, and other things that help to keep the gold absolutely safe.

The United States owns much of the world's gold. And most of the gold we own is in Fort Knox, Kentucky.

Great amounts of silver are also stored away by our government.

Because we have so much gold and silver, our paper money is good. Paper bills, themselves, are not worth anything. But we can use them as money because they are *promises to pay*.

ALL ABOUT OUR PAPER MONEY

Each paper dollar bill has words printed
on it that say our government will pay
a silver dollar for it any time. So the
bill is just as good as the silver dollar
it stands for. This is true for bills of all
amounts.

   Paper money is easier to carry than
metal money. A thousand dollars in
coin would be a great weight. But a
thousand-dollar bill, or two
five-hundred-dollar bills, or ten
one-hundred-dollar bills weigh very
little.

Paper money is made of a very special kind of paper. It has fine threads of red and blue woven into it. If you look at paper money under a magnifying glass you will see these threads.

Counterfeiters try to copy our paper money and coins with the idea of using them for the real thing. The T-men from the United States Treasury Department are always watching for these people and their counterfeit money.

The paper used for our money is made in a secret way. Counterfeiters can't make any exactly like it. Neither can they make exact copies of the designs on paper money. Counterfeit designs are blurred when looked at under a magnifying glass.

Counterfeit coins are more easily noticed than counterfeit bills. Real coins ring when they are dropped. Counterfeit coins make a dull thud. Sometimes they have a greasy feel, too, and usually the lines of their designs are not even and clear.

The designs for paper money are first cut into a master plate of steel by skilled engravers who must be patient and careful. The lines of the designs are very fine and each one must be perfect. It takes several men a long time to make a master plate. From the master plate other plates are made that print the bills.

The printing of paper money is done by machines that print thirty-two bills on each sheet of paper. First the back side of the sheet is printed. When that side has been thoroughly dried and inspected, the face side is printed.

After printing, the bills are coated with a liquid mixture to make them stronger.

The bills are then ironed between rollers.

When they are cut apart the bills are made into neat packages of one hundred bills each.

Great care is used in making paper money. Each bill is checked many times to see that it is perfect. And great care is used, too, to see that no one steals any of the bills before they are sent to the banks.

Paper money gets hard use. It is handled by many people. It is crumpled and wadded. Dirty hands stain it with many things. So it is no wonder worn-out paper money has to be constantly replaced by crisp new bills. One-dollar bills wear out fastest because they are used most. They usually last only about nine months. Five-dollar bills last a year and a half. Other bills last longer.

When old bills are returned to our Treasury they are cut up and destroyed. Then new bills replace them.

MONEY AND BANKS

The Treasury Department sends new money to banks. From the banks it gets to the people.

Banks are important in our lives. They keep our money safe for us in the savings accounts we have talked about. They also lend money when it is needed, but of course they must be sure that the person who borrows is able to repay.

And they have checking accounts, so that people do not have to carry large amounts of money with them. But when Mr. Jones buys something at a store and pays for it with a check, he must

have as much money in the bank as the check calls for. The storekeeper takes the check to the bank and gets cash—bills and coins—for it, or else he deposits the check in his own account. Either way, the money comes out of the money Mr. Jones has in the bank.

When someone writes a check, he is giving the bank orders to pay out some of his money. The check tells the banker to pay the amount of the check from money it is keeping safe for the check-writer.

Cashing checks is just one part of a bank's business. There are many other kinds of business that banks do to help us with money problems.

WHAT MONEY IS

We have seen how money has changed through the centuries, beginning with the early days of bartering. All over the world, every day, different kinds of money are being used. In some places barter still goes on.

If we traveled in other countries we would see many coins that would be strange to us. Some would have holes in the middle. Some would be odd-shaped. They would have words on them that we could not read. But all of them could be exchanged for things or for services. All of them would be a way of measuring the worth of something. Each piece of money would be a symbol of wealth, for that's what money is.

INDEX

Goddesses, as designs for coins, 30
Gods, as designs for coins, 30
gold, for money, 22, 26, 28, 32, 50–51; hoarding of, 32; in America, 50–51; protection of, 50
government, control of coin-making by, 29, 39; money system of, 37
grain, as money, 16, 21
Greece, copper pots used in, 23; metal money of, 24; coin-making in, 30–31

hides, animal, *see* animals, skins of

Iliad, 23
Indians, money of, 19–20
interest, on money, 49

land, products of, for money, 35
lead, as money, 22
leather, cattle for, 13
lumps, of metal, for money, 25, 28

man, ancient, life of, 3–7
marks, on coins, *see* designs
Massachusetts, coins in, 36
meat, trading for, 7; cattle for, 13
metal, for money, 22–32, 40–43; items made of, 22–23; forms of, used for money, 24–26; weight of, 26, 28; value of, 26, 28; mixed, 26, 28, 32, *see also* alloy; *see also individual names of metals*
milk, cattle for, 13
Mints, establishment and location of, 39
molds, for coins, 42–43
money, need for, by cavemen, 3–5; commodities used as, 12–21, 34, 35, *see also individual names of items used for;* metal for, 22–32; coins first used for, 26, 28–33; in America, 34–39; uses of, in Colonial America, 37; use and protection of, 49; importance of, 49; counterfeit, 55; as symbol of wealth, 62; paper, *see* paper money; *see also* coins

necklaces, as money, 18, 22
"New England," stamped on coins, 36
nickel, for coins, 40

"oboli," rods of metal for money, 24
oxen, as money, 13

paper, used for paper money, 54
paper money, first, in Colonial America, 37;

value of, 37, 51; in America, 50–61; printing on, 52; counterfeit, 55; paper used for, 54; designing and making of, 56–58; replacement of, 59
"pieces-of-eight," 34
pigs, as money, 13
planchets, 44–46
pots, metal, as money, 22, 23; clay, 23; three-legged, as prize, 23
promises to pay, paper money as, 37, 51, 52

Revolutionary War, money in, 37
rings, of metal, for money, 25, 26
rods, metal money in shape of, 24–26
Rome, metal money of, 24; coin-making in, 30–32; savage tribes in, 32–33
rubber, as money, 12

salt, as money, 12, 17
sheep, as money, 13, 14
shells, as money, 12, 18–19; *see also specific kinds of shells*
shoes, cattle for purchase of, 14
silver, for money, 22, 26, 28, 31, 32, 36, 40; in America, 50–51
Spain, colonists trade with, 34; silver of, used in American coins, 36
stones, for tools, 3, 7

tea, as money, 12
tigers, teeth of, for money, 20
tin, as money, 22, 40
tobacco, as money, 12, 21; money for, 34
tools, of early days, 3, 7; metal, as money, 22
trading, of tools, 7; and boats, 16; falling off of, 32; resuming of, 33; *see also* barter
tree, as design for coins, 36

United States, *see* America
U.S. Treasury Dep't, and counterfeiters, 55

value, of money, 28, 32, 33, 37, 51
vaults, gold in, 50

wampum, 19, 21
wealth, 62
weapons, metal, as money, 22
weight, of metal, for money, 26; of coins, 28, 29, 53
whales, teeth of, for money, 20
wood, for tools, 7

zinc, for coins, 40

FROM
BARTER
TO GOLD

The Story of Money

by Solveig Paulson Russell

illustrated by Cary

Beginning with the days of the cave men when there was neither money nor the need for it, the author presents the evolution of money in simple terms.

From the development of barter and articles used in trading, Mrs. Russell goes on to explain the history of coins and paper money, and describes current methods of minting and printing. She discusses counterfeit money, and finally offers a short explanation of banking.

Bold, decorative, carefully researched illustrations on every page help to convey the sense of world history that underlies and is, in many ways, responsible for the development of different kinds of money.

P9-ECZ-353

APr